Alexander Buses

GAVIN BOOTH

BRITAIN'S BUSES SERIES, VOLUME 16

Front cover image: One of a growing fleet of Alexander Dennis Enviro400City double-deckers on BYD chassis, a 65-seat 2020 National Express West Midlands bus liveried to promote AD's green credentials. (Keith McGillivray)

Title page image: Posed outside Ottawa's Parliament building, an 86-seat Enviro500 delivered in 2015 to OC Transport of Ottawa.

Contents page image: First has placed many electric buses in its Glasgow fleet, like this 2021 BYD D9UR/AD Enviro200EV, seen in 2022. (Keith McGillivray)

Back cover image: Displaying its oval Alexander Dennis logo next to the registration plate, a new London General two-door 29-seat Enviro200 in Wimbledon in 2007.

Published by Key Books
An imprint of Key Publishing Ltd
PO Box 100
Stamford
Lincs PE9 1XQ

www.keypublishing.com

The right of Gavin Booth to be identified as the author of this book has been asserted in accordance with the Copyright, Designs and Patents Act 1988 Sections 77 and 78.

Copyright © Gavin Booth, 2023

ISBN 978 1 80282 576 3

Typeset by SJmagic DESIGN SERVICES, India.

Contents

Introduction

Like many observers of the bus industry, I still have to remind myself that the giants that dominated the UK bus industry more than 60 years ago are no longer around. The great names I grew up with – AEC, Bedford, Daimler, Duple, Guy and particularly Leyland – are no longer with us as a result of closures, mergers, take-overs and politics. At one time, it was unthinkable that the major players in the 2020s would be an amalgamation of Alexander, Dennis and Plaxton, all builders that have been around for the best part of a century, and in the case of Dennis and Plaxton, much longer, with the roots of Dennis in the late 19th century.

The fact that the Alexander, Dennis and Plaxton names survive, producing buses and coaches for operators not only in the UK but literally across the world, is down to a combination of the right products, tenacity, a global outlook, the ability to bounce back and shrewd management.

I grew up in Scotland, surrounded by buses with bodies built by Alexander, and although Dennis products were comparatively rare up here, that all changed with models like the Dominator and Dart. On the coaching side, for some years Duple products seemed to be everywhere, but gradually Plaxton grew in confidence to emerge as the UK's most important builder of coach bodies.

For Alexander, Dennis and Plaxton, individually and collectively, it has not always been an easy ride and there was a great danger in the early years of this century that these businesses would join so many other great names relegated to the history books.

The images in this book have been selected to show the buses and coaches these companies have built from their early days to today's ever-developing Alexander Dennis (AD) range. Many are my own photos and those, plus many promotional photos issued by the manufacturers, are uncredited. I am happy to acknowledge the assistance I have received from Alexander Dennis and the photographic assistance I have had from Phil Halewood, Keith McGillivray, Sholto Thomas, Richard Walter and from the collections of the late Harry Hay and Julian Osborne. Their images of home and export market buses and coaches have covered gaps in my own travels.

Gavin Booth
Edinburgh

Chapter 1
The Great Survivors

This is the story of three British bus builders that started as family businesses and survived the challenges affecting the industry from the 1980s through to the 2000s to emerge as the strongest force in the British bus industry. The oldest was Dennis, set up in 1895 to manufacture cycles in Guildford, before moving on to motorised vehicles and then bus chassis in 1904. Next was Plaxton, which started building cars in Scarborough in 1907 and moved on to charabanc bodies in the 1920s, recognising the appetite for bus travel in the post-Great War years. Then there was Walter Alexander, who had opened a small cycle shop in Camelon, Stirlingshire, in 1902 and switched to bus operation in 1913. He too recognised the value of building bus bodies for his own fast-growing company, following a few tentative steps in 1924.

The totally separate Alexander, Plaxton and Dennis companies continued to grow. In 1929, the Alexander business became part of the Scottish Motor Traction (SMT) Group, which had benefitted from investment from two of the main-line railway companies, the LMS (the London Midland & Scottish Railway) and the LNER (the London & North Eastern Railway). Soon, Alexander was building buses for other SMT Group companies, as well as for a few smaller independents. Plaxton survived in the busy coachbuilding marketplace with a series of attractive and well-built bodies, often for operators in the north of England. By the same token, Dennis built up a firm following among bus and coach operators in the south-east of England.

In the 1920s and 1930s, none of the three manufacturers would have described themselves as market leaders in terms of output and sales, but they could rely on the quality of their bus chassis and bodies to attract repeat orders. The major players could call on much greater resources and had the ability to satisfy the needs of the largest operators, like London Transport, Birmingham City Transport and other sizeable municipal operators, as well as the British Electric Traction (BET)-group companies throughout England and Wales. They would turn to chassis manufacturers like AEC, Daimler and Leyland, and to bodybuilders like Duple for coaches and Metro-Cammell and Park Royal for buses.

Dennis, which also built lorries and fire engines, was happy to build chassis for orders of any size, which endeared it to many smaller operators, but it also formed a close relationship with the local company operator, Aldershot & District, which bought hundreds of Dennis chassis over a 50-year period.

Plaxton was just one of many coachbuilders catering for the burgeoning tour and hire market, where a competitive price and a well-built, attractive body was the way to win business. The major UK coach body supplier was London-based Duple, which could offer greater capacity. As many smaller coachbuilders fell by the wayside after the first burst of demand for new coaches in the post-World War Two years, Plaxton's reputation spread and with innovative body styles it was soon challenging Duple for the number one spot. In the end it would outlast Duple and emerge as the UK's principal coach bodybuilder.

Alexander had a captive market, building single-deck bus and coach bodies for its fellow SMT Group companies. Leyland, which offered both chassis and bodies, was the favoured supplier for the group's double-deck needs until Alexander introduced its own range of double-deck bodies. And when the SMT Group passed into state control in 1949, the Alexander coachbuilding business remained with the family and started to broaden its horizons, winning orders from bus operators throughout Britain.

For more than 50 years, the Aldershot & District company supported local business by buying Dennis chassis, built just 11 miles away in Guildford. This was a 1923 delivery, a Dennis 4-ton with 32-seat Strachan & Brown bodywork.

At a 1981 launch event, Dennis paraded a selection of new buses, notably the Dominator model that would propel it into the big league of bus builders. Leading the parade are Dominators for South Yorkshire and Leicester, both of which went on to be faithful customers, followed by Greater Manchester and Central Scottish examples. The South Yorkshire and Central buses have Alexander bodies, the Leicester bus has an East Lancs body and the Manchester bus has Northern Counties bodywork.

Dennis was keen to break into the London bus market and supplied three Northern Counties-bodied Dominators to London Transport in 1984; one is seen in Whitehall when new, followed by an Alexander-bodied Volvo Ailsa, another of the test buses purchased to allow in-service comparisons to be made. Although the Dominator did not figure in subsequent London Transport orders, in time Dominators and later Arrows, Lances and particularly Darts and Tridents would be bought for London operations.

Scarborough-based Plaxton enjoyed steady coach body sales for many years, often to operators in the northern part of England and, as here, in Scotland. This Maudslay Marathon III with 33-seat bodywork, delivered in 1947 to Cameron of Arrochar, is typical of Plaxton bodies of that time, built on a variety of chassis.

Left: The cover of a 1996 Plaxton leaflet displays the range of bodywork the company had produced by that time. Oldest is a Ford Model T charabanc built just after the Great War, and there is a side view of a 1952 Venturer, the ground-breaking Panorama, leading up the then current range – a Cresswell Beaver, Nottingham Verde, Shaw Hadwin Premiere, Thamesway Pointer and two early Excaliburs. The leaflet title, Plaxton Profile, anticipates the name given to one of its coach bodies in 2003.

Below: The Volvo B10Ms bodied for Stagecoach in 1995 were the first articulated coaches to be built in Britain and had 71-seat Premiere Interurban bodies.

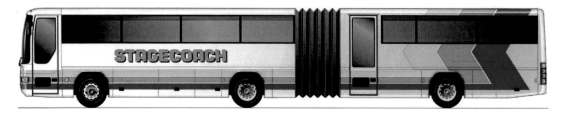

Above: The distinctive lines of a 1930s Alexander coach body. This is a 1934 Leyland Lion LT5B with 32-seat bodywork in the W Alexander fleet.

Right: With its coachworks in Stirling, it made sense for Alexander to pose its products for official photographs with Stirling Castle as a background; here is a 1958 Leyland Tiger Cub with 41-seat dual-purpose body for the W Alexander fleet.

Below: Two Alexander-bodied buses for Arriva Fox County seen in 2000, a recently delivered Volvo B6BLE with 44-seat ALX200 body and a 1998 Mercedes-Benz Vario with 27-seat ALX100 body.

Looking back maybe 60 years, the British bus-building industry was just that: British. Imported chassis and bodies were unknown and the market was dominated by chassis builders like AEC and Leyland, bus bodybuilders like Metro-Cammell and Park Royal, and Duple was the go-to coachbuilder. The idea that in the 21st century, Alexander, Dennis and Plaxton, under the Alexander Dennis banner, would be the principal British-based bus builder, competing with Optare (now Switch Mobility) in Britain and Wrightbus in Northern Ireland and a host of builders from mainland Europe and well beyond, probably never entered the minds of their management or their shareholders.

Before they were united under Alexander Dennis, each of the three main constituent companies can point to a breakthrough model that attracted attention from a much wider range of operators and helped propel them into the mainstream of bus builders.

Back in 1958, it was the Panorama coach body that moved Plaxton into position as a credible rival to market leader Duple. Prompted by BET Group's Sheffield United Tours company, which recognised that coach tour passengers deserved to have larger side windows to enjoy their journeys, Plaxton designers came up with a variation of their existing range with fewer side window pillars, hence longer windows. The Panorama racked up various versions in its 17-year life, with a mixture of facelifts and brand new bodies – coachbuilders liked to keep their ranges looking different and fresh – but all with large side windows as a feature.

For Alexander, which was expanding its customer base, it was the attractive and adaptable Y type that helped it break through into the big league. Its single-deck bus bodies had become well-proportioned but boxy, and Alexander was an early adopter of the use of glass fibre to achieve attractive shapes that were more difficult with metal. The prototype Y types appeared in 1961, perhaps taking a lead from Plaxton by adopting longer side windows, and over the next 21 years, 3,268 Y types were built for Scottish Bus Group companies as well as for operators throughout the United Kingdom. Here was an adaptable

Plaxton's groundbreaking Panorama body, here on a 41-seater on Leyland Tiger Cub chassis from the fleet of Cliff Owen of Chorley, taking part in the North Western Coach Rally in the early 1960s.

body that could be supplied with shorter side windows for service bus work, and longer windows for dual-purpose and coaching work. It was built on a range of chassis from shorter Albions, Bedfords and Fords to legions of 11-metre Leyland Leopards and 12-metre AEC Reliances.

Dennis was still a relatively low-volume bus chassis builder until the appearance in 1977 of the Dominator double-deck chassis, which sold roundly 1,000 chassis in nearly 20 years in production. But it was the single-deck Dart that became a must-have chassis; it went on to become one of the biggest-selling models ever produced in the UK. It had started when Dennis and Duple were both owned by the Hestair Group, and was conceived as an attractive step-entrance midibus in 1988.

This was a time when many operators were still reeling from the after-effects of the deregulation of local bus services in 1986, and needed reliable, attractive and relatively inexpensive buses to compete in the market and protect their territories. At first, the Dart was available as a package with the Dartline body style built by Duple, but the closure of Duple moved Dartline body production to the Carlyle company and by 1991 the Dart chassis was generally available to coachbuilders, notably Alexander, Marshall, Northern Counties, Plaxton and Wright. The Dart was originally conceived for step-entrance bodywork, but from 1995 Dennis offered the SLF (Super Low Floor) version, which helped many operators to invest in low-floor buses for the first time, and the Dart concept still lives on, 20,000 chassis later, in the Alexander Dennis Enviro200 model.

But for the success of the Dart, Alexander, Dennis and Plaxton could well have been names consigned to the history books, alongside AEC, Bristol, Daimler, Duple, Leyland, Metro-Cammell, Park Royal and so many others, and indeed came very close to extinction in the early years of this century. With a successful range of models on offer, Dennis seemed to be destined for a glittering future, particularly

The adaptable Y type single-deck body was a best-seller for Alexander, built on a variety of chassis over a 21-year period. This is a 1967 Eastern Scottish Bedford VAM5 45-seat bus at the gates of Floors Castle in Kelso.

The midi-size rear-engined Dart really cemented Dennis's reputation as a major bus builder. Here was a reliable 8.5m-long lightweight small bus that proved to be adaptable with shorter and longer versions to suit market requirements. This is one of the prototype step-entrance Darts and carries Dennis, Carlyle and Hestair Duple badging on the front, although the distinctively styled 28-seat Dartline bodywork was built by fellow Hestair Group company Duple; this body style was sold to Carlyle. It is here working as a demonstrator to London Buses.

when it planned a merger with Henlys in 1998, which already owned coachbuilder Plaxton. But that relationship was trumped by the Mayflower group when it stepped in to buy the company. Mayflower had acquired coachbuilder Alexander in 1995, the same year that Henlys bought the long-established Northern Counties bodybuilding operation at Wigan. Thus were several of Britain's leading bus-building companies – Alexander, Dennis, Northern Counties and Plaxton – gathered under the Mayflower umbrella.

At first glance this all made sense, particularly when the combination of Mayflower and Henlys morphed into the confident-sounding TransBus International in 2000. But any confidence was short-lived when Mayflower failed and TransBus went into administration in 2004, which could have had a devastating effect on what was left of the home market bus builders. But the future of Alexander and Dennis was saved by a consortium of Scottish businessmen who created Alexander Dennis Ltd in 2004, and while Plaxton was initially sold to its managers, it would be welcomed into the Alexander Dennis fold in 2007.

The fact that Alexander, Dennis and Plaxton survive today under the Alexander Dennis Ltd (AD) banner as by far the largest British-based bus manufacturer is testimony to both the quality of its products and its tenacity against of external factors that could so easily have seen the products of these three proud names disappear in the face of increasing numbers of imported buses and coaches.

This book traces the stories of the three companies that today form Alexander Dennis, looking at their products over the years and their battles for survival when events outside their control took a sudden and dramatic downward turn.

Chapter 2

Dennis

The long-established Dennis company survived the challenges that affected UK-based bus builders and was able to reinvent itself. What had been a respected low-volume builder of bus and coach chassis was suddenly catapulted into the big league in the 1980s with a series of innovative designs that turned out to be exactly what the bus industry was looking for. With the disappearance of major players like Leyland and MCW in the late 1980s, and increased competition from the European mainland, notably from DAF, Scania and Volvo, there was still an appetite for UK-built models that suited UK requirements, which could be very different to those in mainland Europe and beyond; while coach models tended to be more universally acceptable, the UK bus market often looked for something simpler, lighter – and cheaper.

The Dennis story starts in Guildford in 1895, when John and Raymond Dennis set up in business building pedal cycles, soon moving on to simple motorised tricycles and cars and then to buses, the first in 1904. The car market was getting crowded in the early part of the last century and so the decision was made to pull out of cars and concentrate on commercial vehicles. Dennis thus became known for its lorries, buses and fire engines, and while it could never match the quantities that major bus builders like AEC, Daimler and Leyland could offer, it built up a reputation for good engineering that attracted faithful customers around the UK, most notably the locally based Aldershot & District company, which bought a range of Dennis single-deck and double-deck models over a long period, while the Dennis coach chassis range was popular with many independent operators.

The BET Group's Aldershot & District company became a major customer for Dennis chassis, built some 11 miles away. This 1934 trade press advert features one of A&D's Dennis Lancets, with Strachan bodywork.

THE
ALDERSHOT & DISTRICT
  TRACTION CO., LTD.,

who have already taken into service more than 300 Dennis buses, have now favoured us with a Repeat Order which includes

9 Lancets and 1 Lance.

There's nothing like a Dennis except another Dennis!

One of the Aldershot & District Traction Co.'s extensive fleet of Dennis Lancets.

Lancet 4-cylinder chassis for 32-39 seated bodies **£650**

Deferred Terms. Complete 32-seated Dennis-Lancet Bus, £250 deposit and £34 . 16 . 4 per month. Details from Dennis Contracts Ltd., 13, Victoria Street, London, S.W.1.

DENNIS
BROS., LTD., GUILDFORD
Motor Vehicle Manufacturers to H.M. The King.

Aldershot & District came to Dennis in 1954 for a small bus chassis suitable for service in rural areas and the result was the normal control Falcon P5 with 31-seat Strachans body. A&D received 23 of these in 1954/56.

In the 1950s, there was a clear move to underfloor-engined chassis and Dennis introduced its heavyweight Dominant model, but this was quickly abandoned in favour of the lighter Lancet UF, which could not compete with high-volume mainstream models like the AEC Reliance and Leyland Tiger Cub. Dennis dipped a toe in other single-deck markets but with limited success; the Dennis O.6 engine it offered was unfamiliar to many potential customers that were used to AEC, Gardner and Leyland units.

Dennis spotted a gap in the double-deck market in the mid-1950s. Bristol and Eastern Coach Works had developed the Lodekka model, which was a bus to the 'lowbridge' height of slightly over 4m, but without the awkward side gangway upstairs, which previously was the only way bodybuilders could achieve the low height on conventional double-deck chassis. However, only state-owned bus companies could buy the Lodekka, which meant there was a potential market among BET Group companies, as well as municipal and independent operators. Agreement was reached with the British Transport Commission to build the Lodekka under licence, and the Loline was the result, which introduced Dennis models into several important fleets.

But Dennis was not yet really in the big league. Only 280 Lolines were built, at a time when the new breed of rear-engined double-deckers was cornering the market, and Dennis dropped out of the bus market to concentrate on its specialised municipal and fire appliance business.

In 1972, Dennis was taken over by Hestair, which identified potential for a new double-deck model. Leyland now dominated the UK market and was striving to direct its customers to a single model, the Titan, but Hestair recognised that there were operators who were unhappy with Leyland's apparent take-it-or-leave-it approach. In phasing out the popular Fleetline model towards the end of the decade, Leyland was unknowingly creating the opportunity for Hestair Dennis to develop the Dominator. Unlike the Titan, which was available only as a complete standard package, the Dominator offered operators a low-built chassis, often with the tried and tested Gardner 6LX range of engines, that could be completed by bodybuilders around Britain to suit the operator's needs and quirks, although the main UK customer, South Yorkshire PTE, specified Rolls-Royce engines.

Dennis introduced the Lancet UF to compete with the lighter-weight underfloor-engined single-deckers that were coming on to the market at the time. This example, with Strachans body, is on a trade press road test. Although it clearly has the appearance of an Aldershot & District bus, A&D turned to AEC for its single-deckers, but continued to buy Dennis double-deckers.

The Dennis Lancet UF was also chosen as a coach chassis and this 1958 Glenton Tours example has a 32-seat Plaxton Consort front-entrance body.

Left: In 1965, Dennis chose to stop producing buses to concentrate on its other products, but it successfully returned to bus chassis in 1977 with the Dominator, meeting demands from operators for a rear-engined double-decker with the Gardner 6LX family of engines. Over the next 20 years, Dennis produced 1,007 Dominators, including export versions for Hong Kong. This is the 1977 prototype with 77-seat East Lancs body, in Glasgow for demonstration trips when new.

Below: South Yorkshire PTE built up a significant fleet of Dominators between 1978 and 1986. This is a 1983 delivery with Alexander RH type 78-seat body in Sheffield. Although Gardner engines were popular with most Dominator customers, South Yorkshire specified Rolls-Royce Eagle engines.

Many Dominators received bodies built by East Lancs at Blackburn. This is a 1986 76-seat delivery to Southampton Citybus.

The last new trolleybus built in the UK was this 1985 Dominator with Alexander 80-seat Alexander RH type body for South Yorkshire PTE for tests and evaluation. Although it was never able to work in commercial service, it can be seen at the National Trolleybus Museum at Sandtoft, near Doncaster.

GEC, Hestair Dennis and Alexander anticipated the delivery of the South Yorkshire trolleybus with the photo on the cover of this brochure. A photograph of a standard diesel South Yorkshire Dominator has been retouched to include an incorrect registration number, a correct fleet number, and imaginary trolleypoles attached to imaginary overhead.

Roundly 1,000 Dominator chassis were sold, to home market operators as well as into fleets in Hong Kong, and it spawned the less successful single-deck Dominator. The success of the Dominator confirmed that there was clearly a role for Dennis, providing operators with a choice. There was the sturdy front-engined Jubilant for Hong Kong, the Dorchester developed for Scottish Bus Group companies wanting a Gardner-engined bus and coach chassis, the lightweight mid-engined Lancet, and the rear-engined Falcon for operators looking for a latter-day Bristol RE.

Dennis developed the Falcon as a successor to the much-missed Bristol RE chassis. This 1983 Alder Valley Falcon HC with Wadham Stringer Vanguard 49-seat body is leaving London's Victoria Coach Station in 1984, wearing a version of National Bus Company's local coach livery.

Hestair then dabbled in the midibus market with the chunky Domino, but a change of ownership led to the emergence of Dennis as a major player in the bus market. A management buy-out from Hestair in 1988 created Trinity Holdings and from a new factory in Guildford emerged the model that confirmed the role of Dennis as a major player in the bus market – the Dart, a lightweight midibus, available in a range of lengths, that went on to sell almost 3,500 chassis over the next decade. The Dart was joined by the longer Lance model, which played its part in the move away from step-entrance buses to accessible low-floor models when Dennis supplied the SLF (Super Low Floor) version, mainly to London operators, in 1993/94. This in turn led to the introduction of the hugely successful Dart SLF chassis in 1996.

Right: **The Dennis Domino was a sturdy heavy-duty midibus that was only bought by the Greater Manchester and South Yorkshire PTEs. Two of the 1986 Manchester buses, with 24-seat Northern Counties bodies, pick up passengers at Piccadilly bus station on the flat-fare Centreline service.**

Below: **An early example of what turned out to be Dennis's best-selling Dart, a 1990 28-seat delivery to London United, seen in 1994 displaying Carlyle.**

The 1992 prototype Lance with Alexander PS type 52-seat body passed to Go Gateshead in Newcastle in 2000. Behind it are a Go Gateshead Dennis Dart SLF/Plaxton and a Stagecoach Scania N113CRB/Alexander PS type.

This Dennis Lance, with distinctive Northern Counties Paladin 37-seat body, was new to Metroline in London in 1993. Eight years later it had passed to The Birmingham Coach Company, as seen in central Birmingham.

Above: The Lance was popular in Yorkshire and two Lances are seen in Leeds – a 1996 delivery with 49-seat Plaxton Verde body new to Yorkshire Rider and here with First Leeds, pursued by a 1993 Arriva Yorkshire example with 47-seat Alexander Strider body.

Right: Dennis developed the Arrow in 1996, essentially a 10.5m-long double-deck version of the Lance, but low-floor double-deckers were waiting in the wings, and fewer than 100 Arrows were built. The main customer was Capital Citybus, and this is a 1996 delivery with 80-seat Northern Counties Palatine II body, liveried for the East London Line Replacement service.

Dennis recognised that UK operators would not all be looking for the expensive and heavier-weight low-floor single-deck chassis that were likely to be imported from Europe, so introduced the Lance SLF in 1993. This is a 1994 early production model with 34-seat Wright Pathfinder 320 two-door body for CentreWest's Uxbridge Buses operation in London, trumpeting the advantages of low-floor buses.

Other early deliveries of the Lance SLF had Dutch-built Berkhof 2000 NLF 40-seat bodies and went to Stagecoach's East Kent company in 1994. Liveried for Park & Ride work, it still carried a Dutch registration when photographed prior to delivery to the UK.

Over the years, manufacturers and operators have looked at fuels other than diesel for their buses, and this is a 1996 Plaxton Pointer-bodied Dennis Dart converted to run on Compressed Natural Gas (CNG) for First's Cityline fleet in Bristol.

It had quickly become clear to Dennis that what UK operators really wanted was a low-floor version of its successful Dart chassis, and in 1996 the Dart SLF (Super Low Floor) was introduced. It quickly became the most popular chassis, available in a range of lengths. Here Dart SLF production is in full swing at the Dennis plant in Guildford.

This is a significant bus for Dennis and Plaxton – the very first low-floor Dart SLF/Pointer delivered to a customer. Thamesway of Basildon received this 37-seat bus early in 1996.

The Dennis Dart SLF was also bodied by Caetano with its Compass body. This 2001 example was delivered to Burton of Haverhill, and is seen in 2008 in Colchester after the business was sold to Tellings-Golden Miller.

Dennis returned to the coach market in 1987 with the underfloor-engined Javelin chassis. This sold well, often to operators that had previously bought lighter-weight chassis from Bedford and Ford, after both withdrew from the bus and coach market in the mid-1980s.

The Dennis story seemed to be set for a happy ending, but that nearly didn't happen in the difficult years at the start of this century. With a successful range of models selling throughout the UK and to a growing list of export markets, the future had seemed secure, but the problems that followed the collapse of Mayflower in 2004 could have consigned Dennis to the long list of UK bus builders that failed to survive the complex machinations of the manufacturing industry. That Dennis did survive was down to a far-sighted group of businessmen who recognised the need for a strong UK presence in the bus market and ensured that the proud Dennis name survived. Although Dennis chassis are no longer built at its hometown of Guildford, the engineering expertise that created iconic models like the Dart and Trident is still very much a major part of the Alexander Dennis range, which is now built at Falkirk and Scarborough.

AD still has a presence in the south of England with its new Trident House facility in Farnborough, which opened in 2022. Launching the new facility, AD said that it 'will be critical to taking forward the company's new product development agenda and zero-emission mobility ambitions, with the innovative hub housing experts from across the business in aftermarket, engineering and test and development, as well as other key business teams who will underpin future success for the company'. The Trident House name is a nod to the Dennis Trident that introduced so many operators throughout the world to low-floor double-deck chassis.

Dennis's medium-weight Javelin, first introduced in 1987, was a steady seller. This 1996 Javelin GX example with Plaxton Premiere 350 44-seat body was new to South Wales and is here liveried for the National Express Rapide operation.

Chapter 3
Plaxton

The Plaxton business can be traced back to 1907, when Frederick William Plaxton set up in Scarborough as a joiner, quickly moving on to more ambitious building ventures including timber-framed motor car bodies. After the Great War, Plaxton moved up to building charabanc bodies on a variety of chassis and, when charabancs became less popular, turned to fully enclosed 'all-weather' coach bodies. Many of these bodies were built for operators in the north-east of England and Yorkshire, at a time when there were many small coachbuilders throughout Britain competing for business.

Plaxton developed a distinct and stylish design of body in the 1930s, built on a wide range of chassis types and sizes, and also rebodied existing chassis. Plaxton's flair for good coach design helped build the business, but the outbreak of war in 1939 abruptly ended coach production and the Plaxton factory in Scarborough was turned over to producing wooden structures including munitions boxes.

After the war, Plaxton wasted no time in getting back to coachbuilding. New Plaxton-bodied coaches appeared in 1946, again on a range of small and full-size chassis, all front-engined at the time, and these were for a growing list of customers, including familiar names like Excelsior of Bournemouth, Cotter of Glasgow and Wallace Arnold of Leeds. They often won repeat business from a faithful group of customers.

However, bus and coach chassis were changing. The development of chassis with horizontal underfloor engines marked a major step change, and this coincided with a relaxation of overall length regulations

New in 1947, this Foden PVSC6 with 32-seat Plaxton body was used on tour company Strachan's service linking Ballater and Aberdeen. (R L Wilson)

Like most other coachbuilders at the time, Plaxton was able to rebody older chassis with bodies that looked more up to date. This re-registered 1948 Daimler CVD6 received a Plaxton Venturer 39-seat full-fronted body in 1953, and is seen with Ian Glass, Haddington.

that allowed single-deckers up to 30ft (9.14m) long and 8ft (2.44m) wide, where previously 27ft 6in (8.38m) and 7ft 6in (2.28m) had been the maximum. For coach operators, this meant up to 41 seats were possible, rather than 33 or 35, with obvious implications for revenue from passengers. For a time, operators who were cautious about the new chassis stuck to front-engined models, often with full-width fronts as a concession to modernity, but underfloor engines won the day for heavier chassis, while Bedford and Commer, and later Ford, continued to produce lighter-weight front-engined models.

Plaxton tested the new market with its Crusader body, but enjoyed more success with the Venturer, which remained in production from 1950 to 1955 with a number of facelifts along the way. The Venturer was replaced by the Consort, which in 1957 was joined by a service bus body, the Highway, which was often bought by fleets that already included Plaxton coaches.

Plaxton took luxury coach design a giant step further with the Panorama body, introduced in 1958 and featuring three long side windows to give passengers maximum vision. The Panorama was in production for ten years, with regular updates and facelifts – like the UK car industry, coachbuilders believed that customers responded favourably to regular facelifts. The equivalent short-windowed Plaxton model at the time was the Consort and later the Embassy. By this time, underfloor-engined coaches normally had entrances ahead of the front axle where centre entrances had originally been favoured. From 1961, these bodies could be up to 36ft (11m) long.

The Panorama was succeeded in 1968 by the Panorama Elite with curved side windows. Although it was mainly built on underfloor-engined chassis, this also appeared on the new breed of rear-engined chassis, including the Bristol RE and Daimler Roadliner. From 1968, length regulations were relaxed to allow 12m (39ft 4in) long buses and coaches.

Like many coachbuilders based on the British coast, there was a lull in production after Easter each year when operators had taken delivery of their new season coaches and, like some of its competitors, Plaxton used the opportunity to build service bus bodies. There was the metal-framed Derwent in 1962, followed by a very different composite-bodied Derwent in 1966 that was built over a number of years.

A 1956 Leyland Royal Tiger Worldmaster for Ellen Smith, Rochdale, with 41-seat Plaxton Venturer body; the Ellen Smith logo echoes Leyland's Royal Tiger badge on the front.

Inside the Plaxton coachworks in 1960 with a range of coaches including, on the right, a 41-seat Consort on AEC Reliance chassis for Ribblesdale Batty-Holt.

Above: Plaxton built one-off coach bodies for smaller operators and could also supply the needs of the main coach tour companies looking for larger batches. All lined up and ready to go in 1958 are eleven 41-seat Plaxton Consort-bodied Leyland Tiger Cubs for Smith of Wigan, displaying a range of tour destinations as diverse as Ilfracombe and Montreux.

Right: Leyland was proud of its recently introduced Leopard chassis, and chose a Plaxton Embassy-bodied example to illustrate this 1962 trade press advert.

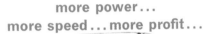

29

Above: Bedford's solution to perfecting a lightweight 11m-long chassis was the twin-steer VAL, and this 1964 VAL14 with Plaxton 49-seat body of Moxon, Oldcotes, is demonstrating its manoeuvrability. Although clearly a member of the Panorama family, these six-wheelers were often badged 'Val'.

Left: The Panorama was restyled in 1965, as on this 51-seat 1967 Daimler Roadliner SRC6 for Blue Bus of Willington. The Roadliner proved to be a troublesome chassis and few were built as coaches.

The next Plaxton coach body range was named Supreme – arch-rival Duple had its Dominant range, so naming new designs became important. The Supreme appeared in 1975 and by 1978 was an all-steel structure, built on a range of chassis, including Mercedes-Benz for UK customers and Ford for export. One less popular version of the Supreme had shallower flat glass side windows.

The Supreme was replaced by the Paramount in 1982, available in standard height (Paramount 3200) and the newly fashionable high-floor (Paramount 3500) version. A double-deck Paramount 4000 was added in 1984, the model names signifying the body height in millimetres. Plaxton now had the confidence and capacity to tender for an increasing range of export coach and bus bodies, often in kit form. There was also a new bus body, the Bustler, in 1980.

Under National Bus Company ownership, new coaches were bought for the Green Line network of coach services linking London with destinations around and beyond the city boundaries. This recently delivered 1977 AEC Reliance with 53-seat Plaxton Panorama Supreme body is picking up passengers on London's Eccleston Bridge on the 707 service to Luton Airport.

This 1975 Bedford YRQ 45-seater for Braybrooke of Mendlesham displays the curved profile to good advantage.

Reeve Burgess was a successful bodybuilder specialising in smaller buses and coaches. Eastern Scottish bought five of these Reeve Burgess-bodied 13-seat Bedford CF350 for the innovative Border Courier service in 1979. The buses linked local health centres in the Scottish Borders with the main hospital, and featured a lockable rear compartment in which prescriptions and medicines could be stored. In 1980, Plaxton bought the Reeve Burgess business.

Following coach service deregulation in Britain in 1980, several new ventures were set up to take advantage of this new freedom. One was British Coachways, an ambitious but short-lived consortium of coach operators running under a common brand. At London Heathrow Airport in 1981 is a 1980 Excelsior DAF MB200 with Plaxton Panorama Supreme IV 53-seat body. Behind it is a Green Line Leyland Tiger with arch-rival Duple's curved-profile Dominant body.

Plaxton's first double-deck body was the Paramount 4000, introduced in 1984. This is a Yorkshire Traction 71-seater on Neoplan N722 chassis for National Express's upmarket Rapide services between Yorkshire and London.

A 53-seat Plaxton Paramount 3500, new in 1990 to Lowland Scottish, is in Chieftain Tours livery on a Scania K113CRB chassis.

Plaxton had started on the takeover trail in 1980 when in acquired the Reeve Burgess business, which specialised in smaller buses and coaches. Then in 1986, it bought Kirkby, the major coach dealer, and three years later came the purchase of Henlys, principally a car dealer with car and coach-building interests. Plaxton's greatest rival, Duple, closed in 1989 and this cemented Plaxton's place as the UK's principal coach body builder, with an increasing output of bus bodies from Scarborough and from Reeve Burgess. In 1991, the Reeve Burgess factory was closed and production of two increasingly popular models was transferred to Scarborough – the Beaver minibus, mostly on Mercedes-Benz chassis, and the Pointer midibus on the Dennis Dart.

These successes in the bus market led to the introduction of the Plaxton Verde body for full-size single-deck bus chassis in 1991, the same year it announced its new coach body range – the Premiere and Excalibur. The Premiere was available in two versions, suffixed 320 or 350 according to height, while the Excalibur had a more streamlined front end and was available only in 3.5m-high form. Both designs marked a move away from the big side windows pioneered by the Panorama in 1958. The shallower flat glass allowed the designs to meet European roll-over regulations as manufacturers and operators became more safety-conscious.

There was also a move to low-floor models, and a low-floor version of the Pointer was introduced in 1995 for Dennis Dart SLF and Volvo B6LE chassis. The Dart SLF/Pointer was a runaway success and allowed many operators to move to reasonably priced low-floor (technically low-entry) models. While European operators have tended to favour fully low-floor single-deckers, the UK market has largely stuck to the less complex low-entry types with the low-floor section ahead of the rear axle, and steps to the rear leading to the remainder of the seating.

Henlys acquired the Northern Counties coachbuilding business in 1995. Principally a bus builder, Northern Counties offered an inheritance of single-deck and double-deck body styles, but its factory at Wigan became the home of the successful President low-floor double-deck body, badged as a Plaxton.

Plaxton's stylish new Verde bus body first appeared on this Scania N113CRB demonstrator in 1991.

Two Stagecoach Ribble 1994 Dennis Javelins with Park Royal Premiere 47-seat bodies pass in central Manchester in 1995, working on the Mancunian network of limited-stop services.

Dual-door Plaxton Pointer-bodied Dennis Darts were rare outside London, but Thames Transit took some 37-seat examples in 1995.

The increasingly close relationship between Dennis and Plaxton led to the announcement of a merger in 1998, but the Mayflower group made a better offer and gained control of Dennis. Mayflower already owned the Walter Alexander coachbuilding business.

A new Plaxton coach body range appeared in 1999 – the standard Paragon and flagship Panther – and the choice of coach bodies has expanded further since. The Panther has been joined by the midi-size Panther Cub and more recently the low-entry Panther LE for limited-stop and shorter express services. The popular Elite body, launched in 2008 as a top-of-the-range flagship model, has spawned the Elite i interdeck coach and there is a version of the Elite for New Zealand. For local coach work there is the Leopard, and for capacity there is the double-deck Panorama, this name recalling the trend-setting design that launched Plaxton into the big league in 1958.

More than 20 years after TransBus threatened to close Plaxton's Scarborough plant, it is thriving as an important part of the AD family, producing coach and bus bodies for a growing list of customers.

Left: Plaxton continued to body Mercedes-Benz Vario chassis with the Beaver 2 body – this is a 1997 27-seater for First's PMT fleet.

Below: The Plaxton Primo was a minibus model developed with Enterprise Bus and assembled in Hungary for completion at Scarborough. This 28-seat demonstrator is in Hamilton bus station in 2006, on loan to Whitelaw of Stonehouse.

Chapter 4
Alexander

In the early years of the 20th century, hundreds of entrepreneurs recognised the potential for motor bus services but, inevitably, many misjudged the market or lacked the business acumen to survive. Others were mopped up – often willingly – by the more ambitious companies. The Alexander bus-operating business started in central Scotland and had grown sufficiently by 1924 to appreciate the value of building bus bodies for its own fleet. In 1929, the Alexander bus business, including its growing bodybuilding department, had become part of the SMT Group, which grew in the 1930s to become a major Scottish bus operator alongside the municipal fleets. The Alexander body shop at Stirling was kept busy building single-deck bus and coach bodies for its own use and for its sister SMT Group companies.

The first Alexander-built bodies were fairly utilitarian, but as the coachbuilding side expanded, the designers developed a range of stylish bodies that were clearly recognisable as Alexander bodies. These were solidly built buses and stylish coaches that compared well with the products of the major bodybuilders of the time.

The first Alexander double-deck bodies appeared in 1942, during World War Two and initially to a Leyland pre-war design, but from 1943 there was a utility lowbridge design on rebodied AEC and Leyland chassis for SMT fleets, as well as a normal-height configuration for Glasgow Corporation in 1944 to rebody older AEC Regents. After the war, Alexander returned to normal production with upgraded

Alexander bodies of the 1930s were mounted on a range of chassis. This 1929 Leyland Tiger TS2 with 1934 Alexander 32-seat bus body is now preserved.

Stirling Castle provided an impressive backdrop to many Alexander official photographs. This is a 1938 AEC Regal 34-seat bus with typically Scottish cutaway rear entrance and roof-mounted luggage rack for the SMT fleet.

versions of its pre-war designs, but in 1949 the coachbuilding arm was retained by the Alexander family when the Alexander bus-operating business and the other SMT Group companies were sold to the state-owned British Transport Commission, creating what became the Scottish Bus Group (SBG).

Walter Alexander & Co (Coachbuilders) Ltd continued to supply its existing customers, which were now part of SBG, and started to look for business in Scotland and in other parts of Britain. It won orders from the municipal fleets at Aberdeen, Dundee, Edinburgh and Glasgow, from English and Welsh municipalities and eventually from BET Group companies and independent operators throughout England, thanks to the new purpose-built Falkirk plant, which opened in 1958 and is still the heart of the business.

Alexander's flair for good design blossomed in the 1960s, often making good use of glass fibre to achieve shapes that would have been difficult with aluminium. The classic and apparently infinitely adaptable Y type and A type ranges used steel and later aluminium structures that offered different side window layouts, different front-end window styles and designs, and peaked or rounded domes on double-deckers, giving customers the bodies that best suited their needs and tastes. So much so that other builders, notably East Lancs and other coachbuilders to a lesser degree, produced double-deck bodies that bore more than a passing resemblance to current Alexander designs. For the new breed of rear-engined single-deck chassis, it developed the W type bus body, and for SBG's prestigious Scotland–London services there was the 12m-long M type with smaller double-glazed side windows, transatlantic-style.

The double-deck A type and single-deck Y type were initially steel-framed bodies, but Alexander was moving on to aluminium alloy-framed buses in the 1970s with the introduction of the AL and AY types.

The first double-deck bodies built by Alexander were to Leyland design. This was a 1942 delivery to the SMT company, a low-bridge 53-seater on Leyland Titan TD5 chassis. It is now preserved.

The first Alexander bodies on the new underfloor-engined single-deck chassis were 30-seat AEC Regal IVs with toilets for Scottish Bus Group's Scotland–London services in 1951. A convoy of these from the Scottish Omnibuses fleet heads towards Edinburgh when new.

Alexander developed this rounded double-deck body design in the 1950s, here in low-bridge 53-seat form on a 1953 Leyland Titan PD2/12 for the W Alexander fleet, and now preserved.

The Alexander lightweight coach design was built for customers in Scotland and England. This 1954 Leyland Tiger Cub 41-seater was supplied to Barton, Chilwell, in 1954.

Above: This straight-waisted design was supplied in bus and dual-purpose form. Carmichael of Glenboig, trading as Highland – and not to be confused with Scottish Bus Group's Highland company – bought this Leyland Leopard L1 45-seat bus in 1961.

Right: Alexander adapted its double-deck design to suit low-height chassis, notably the Albion Lowlander. This 1963 LR1 model has a 72-seat C type body for the Central SMT fleet. Behind it is a 1956 Glasgow Corporation AEC Regent V, again with Alexander bodywork, although this was built to a Weymann design. (Harry Hay)

The majority of Alexander bodies on rear-engined double-deck chassis were to normal height, but customers were looking for a low-height version, and this was the D type on Daimler Fleetline and Leyland Atlantean chassis. The first D type was this 1963 73-seater for Scottish Omnibuses.

The Alexander Y type, which first appeared in 1961, was sold to a wide variety of customers in different forms. This big-windowed version was a popular choice, as here on an 11m-long 1967 AEC Reliance 49-seater for the BET Group's Potteries company.

In 1968, the Scottish Bus Group came to Alexander for a new design of 12m-long body for its Scotland–London services, and the result was the M type with its small double-glazed side windows and external ribbing. Two newly completed M type 42-seaters on Leyland Leopard chassis for SBG's Fife and Northern fleets sit outside the Alexander coachworks in Falkirk in 1975.

The assembly line at Alexander's Falkirk coachworks in May 1976, with, furthest from camera, lines of D type bodies on Daimler Fleetline chassis for Scottish Bus Group, then T type Leyland Leopards, again for SBG, AL type Atlanteans for the Glasgow and Edinburgh municipal fleets, and, nearest camera, more SBG T types.

The AY was largely visually similar to the original Y type, but the opportunity was taken to redesign the double-deck body, which emerged as the deeper-windowed AL type, still infinitely adaptable to suit the preferences of its customers.

In 1969, Walter Alexander & Co (Belfast) was founded to acquire the Potters (Belfast) coachbuilding business. Potters had previously been sub-contracted to build Y type bodies on Albion Viking chassis for use by the three Alexander fleets in Scotland, and there were strong hints of Alexander design in other Potters bodies. As Alexander (Belfast), it continued to supply the Northern Ireland market, often with designs that were specific to that market. In addition to the major operators, Ulsterbus and Belfast Corporation, it built school buses, fire appliances, ambulances and other municipal vehicles. It also built Y type bodies for Scottish Bus Group operations, to relieve pressure on the Falkirk coachworks, and some designs developed for Ulsterbus and its sister Citybus were bought by operators on the British mainland.

In 1975, Alexander dipped a tentative toe into the export market, building bodies and fabricating kits for local assembly overseas. As its competitors fell by the wayside, Alexander was well placed to win substantial orders from an expanding range of customers and countries.

The 1980s were difficult years for coachbuilders, as many bus operators held back from investing in orders for larger vehicles until they had assessed the impact of the deregulation of coach and bus services outside London and the privatisation of state-owned and municipal companies that followed. In the mid-1980s, Alexander produced large numbers of minibus bodies and conversions, but bounced back with the PS type single-deck body, successor to the Y type, and a new range of bodies that had type names for the first time – there was the Sprint minibus body, the midi-size Dash for Dennis and Volvo chassis, the big single-deck Strider, built on Dennis, Scania and Volvo chassis, and the Ultra body, built in Belfast on Volvo B10L chassis. Alexander (Belfast) produced the Setanta body on DAF and Volvo chassis for Bus Éireann.

Sitting outside the Alexander coachworks in Falkirk in 1979, awaiting collection, are two 74-seat buses with AL type bodies – a South Yorkshire PTE Leyland Atlantean with peaked-dome body and a Leyland Fleetline with rounded dome for the Bournemouth municipal fleet.

The Alexander Y type body in AYS 53-seat bus form usually had shorter side windows, like this 1980 Eastern Scottish Seddon Pennine 7 at Hawick in a livery promoting the company's Scotland–London services, which used considerably more comfortable vehicles than this.

In its efforts to find a new standard double-deck model, London Transport took small batches of different types to be tested in service. A 1984 front-engined Volvo Ailsa with two-door Alexander RV type 78-seat body is seen in 1985.

In 1990, the Alexander business had been sold to Spotlaunch, then to its management two years later, and then to Mayflower in 1995; an unfortunate move, perhaps, when you consider what would develop over the next decade.

Deregulation of British bus services outside London in the 1980s led to a fall in orders for new double-deck buses and companies like Alexander were forced to turn to minibus bodies and conversions. High above Brighton when new is a 1985 Brighton & Hove Mercedes-Benz L608D with Alexander AM 20-seat body.

The fast-growing Stagecoach company bought many Alexander bodies and one of the more unusual was the Magicbus Megadekka, the 1989 three-axle Leyland Olympian proclaiming itself to be Britain's Biggest Bus, with 110 seats in its RL type body – achieved by a certain amount of three-and-two seating. It is photographed here outside the Alexander Falkirk plant.

The Belfast-built Alexander Q type body was mainly built for the Ulsterbus/Citybus fleets in Northern Ireland. This 1991 Citybus 51-seater on Leyland Tiger is in Belfast in 1996.

Right: Alexander RH type 78-seat bodywork on a Scania N113DRB chassis for East London in 1991.

Below: The first and only articulated bus bodied by Alexander was this Mercedes-Benz O405 three-door 60-seater for Grampian Transport in 1992.

The Dash body was designed for the increasingly popular midi-size chassis, and this is a 1993 40-seat Dash on Volvo B6 chassis for Stagecoach's Cumberland fleet, in Carlisle.

Another named Alexander model was the Strider. This 1993 SMT Lothians Volvo B10B/Strider 51-seater is in Edinburgh, followed by a rare underfloor-engined Leyland Lion from the same fleet, a 1986 bus with Alexander RH type 86-seat body.

This 1995 9.8m-long Dennis Dart with 40-seat Dash body started life in the Yorkshire Rider fleet, but by 2008 it had been transferred to First in Portsmouth.

Alexander became involved in the diesel multiple-unit railcar business in the mid-1980s, when demand for buses had fallen following deregulation. In conjunction with Hunslet-Barclay, it produced bodies for 25 two-car Pacers in 1985/86 for British Rail, and this is the first, 143001, at the Kilmarnock factory of Andrew Barclay. Alexander subsequently produced bodies for the 23 similar Class 144 Pacers.

Chapter 5
The Mayflower Years

By 1995, the three bus builders that would go on to form Alexander Dennis were growing in confidence and importance. They had survived the major upheavals in the UK-based bus-building industry that changed the shape of it for ever.

In 1962, Leyland had started the process when it bought AEC, and that set in train the sequence of events that led to the political shenanigans that created state-owned British Leyland. Leyland also mopped up chassis builders Bristol, Daimler and Guy and bodybuilders Eastern Coach Works, Park Royal and Roe, before a 1986 management buyout and subsequent sale of the remains of Leyland's bus-building empire to Volvo two years later. This meant that the coast was clear for Alexander, Dennis and Plaxton to emerge as cornerstones of the UK bus industry, but the years between 1990 and 2004 would see changes in ownership that affected and ultimately threatened the long-term future of these respected names.

Dennis was building more bus chassis than ever before as orders poured in for its Dart. The Hestair connection was severed in 1988 by a management buyout that created Trinity Holdings. Fast forward ten years and Dennis and Plaxton, which were working closely producing the best-selling Dart range, announced a merger. However, they were beaten to the draw by Mayflower, which tabled a higher bid for Dennis, which was accepted. It quickly sold the Dennis Eagle refuse collection arm, concentrating instead on bus and coach chassis and fire appliances.

Plaxton had bought coachbuilder Reeve Burgess in 1980, prominent bus and coach dealers Kirkby in 1986, the French coachbuilder Carrosserie Lorraine in 1988 and motor dealer Henlys in 1989, which in turn bought the Northern Counties bodybuilding business in 1995. In 1989, Plaxton's arch-rival Duple had closed, so Plaxton had seemed to be in a strong position through a mixture of good design, market awareness, well-built buses and coaches and the external factors that had changed the face and shape of the UK bus-building industry.

While all this was happening, the Mayflower engineering group bought the Walter Alexander business from its management buyout team. The Alexander family had withdrawn from its coachbuilding business in 1990, selling it to Spotlaunch, which in turn led to a management buy-out in 1992. This was the situation until Mayflower bought the business in 1995.

Under Mayflower, the ALX range of Alexander body types emerged. Between 1996 and 1998 it introduced the ALX100 minibus, the ALX200 midibus, the full-size single-deck ALX300 and the double-deck ALX400. The ALX200 was discontinued in 2002 and a Pointer line was established at Falkirk.

In 2000, Mayflower and the spurned Henlys business created a joint venture, TransBus International, with 70 per cent owned by Mayflower to Henlys' 30 per cent. On the surface, with Alexander, Dennis and Plaxton now in common ownership there seemed to be strength in numbers and a start was made to discontinue duplicated models and create new model ranges. Inevitably, TransBus set about rationalising, with an announcement that the Plaxton Scarborough plant was to be closed and the Alexander coachworks at Falkirk would move to nearby Larbert. Neither happened, but from 2001 TransBus did introduce the first models in a new range of low-floor bus types – the full-size single-deck Enviro300 and the three-axle export double-deck Enviro500.

Above: The Plaxton Prestige body had started out as a Northern Counties product, the Wigan-built Paladin LF, but Plaxton continued to produce it at Scarborough into the Mayflower era as the Prestige. Arriva was a major customer and this is a 1998 45-seat Prestige on DAF SB220 chassis for Arriva Tees.

Right: The cover of this 1995 Alexander promotional brochure is entitled *New Horizons* and shows Walter Alexander Ltd as 'A member of the Mayflower Corporation plc'. It uses images of home market bodies – an AM type minibus, a Dash, a PS type, a Strider, a Royale, a Belfast-built Ultra, and a Strider for Singapore and a Royale for Hong Kong.

Two new Alexander-bodied Volvos delivered to competing operators in 1997 – a Greater Glasgow Olympian with 79-seat RL type body and a Stagecoach B10M PS type 49-seater.

The 24-hour Oxford–London service provided by the Oxford Bus Company was regularly updated with new coaches. This Volvo B10M with Plaxton Excalibur 53-seat body was delivered in 1998, carrying an appropriate registration mark.

First Beeline bought three-axle Volvo B12Ts with 51-seat Plaxton Excalibur bodies in 1999 for the busy Rail-Air service linking Reading and London Heathrow Airport.

The Dennis R series was a premium coach chassis introduced in 1999 and is seen here with a Plaxton Paragon 49-seat body delivered in 2001 to Don Prentice, Haddington.

The Alexander Ultra body was built in its Belfast plant on Volvo B10L chassis to a Volvo design, under licence. This 43-seat example was new to National Express West Midlands in 1997, and is seen in Birmingham in 2010.

Left: With just the Plaxton logo but no visible manufacturers' names, this is a 2000 Volvo B10M with Plaxton Panther 50-seat body for the important Shearings coaching company.

Below: A 2002 delivery to Weardale, Stanhope, a three-axle Volvo B12T with 49-seat Plaxton Excalibur body.

Although Stagecoach standardised on Alexander-built bodies for its Dennis Trident fleet, it turned to Plaxton in 2003 for low-height President 78-seat bodies for its Manchester operation; by 2011 this one was working for Stagecoach in Hull, liveried for the Frequento service.

Right: Outside London, Lothian was the main customer for the Plaxton President body, and this 11.4m-long 83-seat example was delivered in March 2004, the same month the Mayflower Group went into administration.

Below: Some existing models were re-badged, so strictly this is a Stagecoach TransBus Dart with TransBus Pointer 38-seat body, seen when new in Coventry in 2004, although it is still recognisable as a Dennis/Plaxton product, and in Stagecoach fashion it displays no manufacturer badging.

The full-size Enviro300 was launched in 2001, in the TransBus years. Seen in 2018, this is a 2004-vintage 40-seat delivery to Cardiff Bus with the original frontal styling.

Some of these new models had not yet gone into production when Mayflower, and consequently TransBus, went into administration in 2004, followed shortly by Henlys. A prominent industry observer described the uncertainties of the Mayflower/TransBus years as 'the rollercoaster ride of doom', and this could well have been the end of the road for the Alexander, Dennis and Plaxton brands, but the cavalry arrived in the form of a group of Scottish investors who bought Alexander and Dennis and created Alexander Dennis Ltd (AD), while Plaxton passed to a management buy-out. So AD survived with plants at Guildford (Dennis) and Falkirk (Alexander). AD did not, however, buy the Alexander (Belfast) business based at Mallusk in Northern Ireland.

Henlys had bought the Northern Counties bus-building business in 1995, which was mainly producing the successful President body under the Plaxton name, but the Wigan plant closed in 2005 after briefly passing into Alexander Dennis ownership. In 2007, Alexander Dennis bought Plaxton, bringing the three complementary arms of Britain's biggest bus business under common ownership that would make good use of the synergy that this created.

Chapter 6
The Name Game

Some bus and coach manufacturers seem to have enjoyed finding model names for their products, while others have stuck to type codes composed of letters and numbers that usually make some sense. The three main components of Alexander Dennis – Alexander, Dennis and Plaxton – fall into both camps.

Dennis started with purely descriptive names like 30cwt and 4-ton, and then started working its way through the alphabet; the E, F and G, for example, were 1920s chassis for single-deck buses and coaches to different sizes and configurations. It then started giving its models names, often on a theme of sharp instruments and weapons, which gave us the Arrow, Dart, Javelin, Lance, Lancet, Mace, Pike and Trident; the Trident was a 1990s name, while Arrow, Dart and Lance were used in the 1930s and the names were revived in more recent times. Dennis was also an important builder of fire appliances and some of these had 'sharp' names, like the Dagger, Rapier and Sabre.

Not all Dennis model names followed this pattern. There were animal and bird names – the Condor, Dragon, Falcon and Pelican; and there were the alliterative names, like Dart, Dominant, Dominator, Domino and Dorchester. Some more recent names didn't fit into these categories, like the Jubilant, Loline and R series. And there is another interesting Dennis name: from 1934 the company built housing for its employees in Guildford and the area was named Dennisville.

This was one of 14 similar buses supplied to the Newport municipal fleet between 1954 and 1956 – note the full Dennis Lancet UF badging. The Davies 44-seat body was built on Park Royal frame.

Several of the larger operators chose not to carry manufacturers' names on the fronts or backs of their buses and coaches, but this 1997 Metroline Plaxton Pointer-bodied 30-seat two-door Dennis Dart SLF is only lacking a Dart badge to complete the set.

The Dennis Lance was a full-length (11.5m) rear-engined single-deck chassis developed from the Dart. Dennis commissioned demonstrators to give potential customers the opportunity to try the new chassis. These carried Plaxton Verde and Alexander PS type bodies, and are seen at the Dennis plant in 1992 – the Verde in a perhaps optimistic London-style red and the PS type in SMT green/cream.

Two well-badged Berkhof-bodied Dennis buses in the NZH fleet in the Netherlands – a Dart and a Lance.

Plaxton did not name its models until 1950, when new coach bodies were named Crusader, Envoy and Venturer. Later in the 1950s came the Consort and the innovative Panorama, in 1968 the Panorama Elite and in 1974 the Supreme. Alliterative names really started in 1982 with the Paramount, followed in a rush in the 1990s by the Panther, Paragon, Premiere, Prestige and Prima. This century we have seen the revival of the Elite and Panorama names, joined by Leopard, Panther Cub, Panther LE and Profile.

And these are just the coach bodies. Although the buses built under the Plaxton brand have sometimes used 'P' names, like the Pointer, President, Primo and Pronto, others have carried a range of model names. There was the Highway in the 1950s, the Derwent in various guises between 1952 and 1991, the Beaver and the Bustler in the 1980s, and more recently the Centro and Verde.

This 1972 Plaxton demonstrator is a Ford R1114 with Plaxton's Panorama Elite III body. The Panorama name was a popular one, dating back to 1958, and the Panorama Elite, the first British coach with curved side windows, was built between 1968 and 1975.

The tour company Wallace Arnold was a solid Plaxton customer over many years and this 1996 image contrasts a recently delivered Premiere-bodied 50-seat Volvo B10M with a 1958 41-seat centre-entrance Consort-bodied AEC Reliance.

A 1997 line-up of new Trent deliveries that demonstrates the range of the Plaxton offering. From the left, they are a 40-seat Pointer-bodied Dennis Dart, a 51-seat Premiere-bodied Volvo B10M and a 31-seat Beaver-bodied Mercedes-Benz Vario.

Two 33-seat Plaxton-bodied Mercedes-Benz Varios for TransLinc in 2001. On the left is a Cheetah coach, beside a Beaver 2 bus.

Two Volvo coaches in the fleet of Elcock of Madeley in 2003 illustrate the development of the Plaxton coach range. On the left is a 1988 B10M with 53-seat Paramount body, alongside a newly delivered B12B with Panther body, celebrating the operator's 75th anniversary. The B10M had clocked up more than one million kilometres in 15 years.

Alexander never publicly bothered about model designations until the early 1960s, when an alphabetical body code system was introduced. It was a simple concept – double-deckers started with the A type normal-height body on Atlantean and Fleetline chassis, working its way through the alphabet to the updated L type; single-deckers worked backwards from the Z type, built to the BET standard design, to the M type motorway coach body. When Alexander moved from steel to aluminium alloy construction in the 1970s, the relevant body types gained an 'A' prefix, hence the double-deck AL and single-deck AY.

By the 1980s the A prefix was superfluous, so new models reverted to a basic single letter code, with extra letters added to indicate variations. So the standard double-deck body became the R type, spawning distinctions like the RH for normal height bodies, the RL for low-height bodies and the RDC for a small batch of double-deck coaches. The AY type was replaced by the P type in 1983, which in turn gave way to the more popular PS type in 1988. This was initially restyled for Singapore, hence the added 'S'. The face-lifted dual-purpose single-deck T type became the TC (coach), TE (express) and TS (service bus). The first named models were the single-deck Sprint (minibus), Dash (midibus) and Strider and Ultra (full-size) in the early 1990s, followed by the more rounded Royale double-deck body in 1993. And for the Irish market, there was the Setanta – after a mythological Irish figure.

For its range of bodies for low-floor chassis, Alexander used the prefix ALX, so the ALX200 was a midi-size single-deck body, the ALX300 a full-size single-decker, the ALX400 a two-axle double-decker and the ALX500 a three-axle double-decker. There was also the ALX100 minibus body. These code numbers, apart from the 100, carried on into Alexander Dennis days for the expanding Enviro range, but there is now the Enviro100EV.

Although Alexander normally stuck to letters of the alphabet to distinguish its bodies, the body for the new Dennis Dart and Volvo B6 chassis was given the name Dash. This is a 1996 First Grampian 9.8m Dart with Dash 40-seat body in Aberdeen when new.

Alexander (Belfast) developed the Setanta body for Bus Éireann, which was mounted on Volvo B10B and, as here, DAF SB220 chassis. This is a 1993 two-door 44-seater. Setanta is the given name of the Irish mythological figure Cú Chulainn.

The reworking of the Alexander R type in 1993 was given the name Royale. This is a 1997 Lothian Buses 81-seat two-door Royale-bodied Volvo Olympian.

Chapter 7

Exports

Countries in the Far East played a major part in the export activity of then-separate Alexander and Dennis in the 1970s. Dennis had exported chassis to Hong Kong in the 1920s, but Alexander had been firmly focused on developing its UK business until an enquiry from China Motor Bus (CMB) in 1975 led to the supply of bodies, both built-up and in kit form, for CMB and Kowloon Motor Bus (KMB). These were principally double-deck bodies on a range of chassis including the Daimler Fleetline, Leyland (Guy) Victory, Volvo Ailsa and, unusually, the single-deck Mercedes-Benz O.305.

Singapore Bus Service (SBS) was another early Alexander customer, for double-deck kits on Leyland Atlantean chassis and single-deck kits on Leyland Leopards. Later SBS would take single-deck bodies on Volvo B10M chassis; the PS type was to a style that would subsequently prove popular with British operators, notably Stagecoach.

Involvement in the export business was an astute move for Alexander, which could see the threat to its traditional markets from new integral models like the Leyland National and Leyland Titan, and the phasing out of the Bus Grant scheme, which had provided financial inducements to encourage home-market customers to invest in buses suitable for driver-only operation.

In the meantime, Dennis was producing bespoke rugged double-deck chassis for Hong Kong operators, some with Alexander bodies. There was the front-engined Jubilant and later a three-axle version of its rear-engined Dominator chassis for Hong Kong, named the Dragon (or for CMB, the Condor).

Activity also moved to the African market with sturdy Dennis Dragons for use by Stagecoach operations in Kenya and Malawi. European bus companies wanted the lighter-weight Dart chassis, and these were sold to operators in the Netherlands, Portugal and Spain, with locally built bodywork.

The Hong Kong and Singapore markets have continued to be important for Alexander Dennis, but the net has widened considerably, with a growing list of customers literally from all parts of the world.

An early export order for Alexander was from China Motor Bus (CMB) in 1978, for new bodies on Guy Arab V chassis dating from the 1960s. This version of the Alexander designs of the time was supplied, with full-width front, possibly to disguise the age of the chassis. These were two-door 80-seaters; this example had been rebodied in 1982.

The first two bodies from an order for 22 on left-hand drive Leyland Atlantean chassis for Metro Manila in the Philippines were built at the Alexander coachworks in Falkirk. Here they near completion in 1980, alongside a Tyne & Wear Atlantean. The remaining 20 were assembled in the Philippines, using completely-knocked-down (CKD) kits supplied from Scotland.

Netherlands-based Noord-Zuid-Hollandsche (NZH) bought Dennis Dart and Lance chassis with step-entrance Berkhof bodies in the 1990s. This is a 1996 two-door 41-seat example.

Singapore Bus Service was an early and subsequently important customer for Alexander bodies. This 1986 Leyland Atlantean has 86-seat RHS type bodywork, developed for Singapore. (Julian Osborne)

The first of a batch of Scania L113CRL with Alexander Strider 45-seat two-door body supplied to Trans Island Bus Services (TIBS), Singapore, in 1995/97. The front-end treatment differed from home-market Striders.

The Alexander Dennis Enviro500, aimed initially at well-established markets in the Far East, was beginning to attract attention from places where Alexander's long experience in building double-deck bodies was recognised as an advantage. Enviro500s have been sold to operators in Canada, Germany, Mexico, New Zealand, Switzerland and the United States. There are Enviro500 models tailored to the requirements of operators in Asia, Australasia, North America, Latin America and Europe, as well as a SuperLo and electric EV CHARGE versions for North America.

Initially, Alexander would usually build a prototype at Falkirk, which was shipped out as a master for local assembly of bodies supplied from Falkirk in kit form. In major markets like the Far East, the volume of orders meant that local body assembly became an essential function, and Alexander staff oversaw the build process to ensure that the pace of work and quality standards were maintained.

To meet the demand, Alexander Dennis has developed partnerships around the world and has or has had assembly partners in China, New Zealand and the United States, building single-deck and double-deck bodies to AD designs, many adapted to suit local requirements. So while the Enviro500 three-axle double-decker is popular in many export markets, often introducing the concept of the double-deck bus as an alternative to articulated single-deckers, there are variations, like the 3.9m-high SuperLo version for North America and the three-axle 12.6m-long single-deck Enviro200EV XLB for New Zealand operations.

Nearer home, Alexander has supplied bodies to operators in the Republic of Ireland, initially from its Belfast plant and more recently from Falkirk and Scarborough. These have usually been very similar to bodies supplied to UK customers.

In the Republic of Ireland, Bus Éireann and Dublin Bus have been good customers for Alexander for some years, first with bodies built at the Alexander (Belfast) plant and then at Falkirk and Scarborough. This is a 1995 Dublin Bus Volvo Olympian with 74-seat two-door body in Dublin in 1998.

Aimed at the French market, the 3.7m-high Plaxton Prestige body on Volvo B12R chassis was unusual on two-axle chassis. The Prestige name was also used for a body on low-floor bus chassis for the home market.

One of ten step-entrance Dennis Darts with 32-seat two-door Plaxton Pointer bodies that were in service with Transmac in Macau in 1996.

CityFlyer, a brand of Hong Kong operator Citybus, was set up in 1998 to serve the new Hong Kong International Airport, and initially used Dennis Tridents with 78 coach-seated Duple Metsec two-door bodies finished by Caetano.

Looking very similar to Alexander ALX200-bodied Dennis Dart SLFs delivered to Arriva's UK fleets, this left-hand drive example in Groningen is one of 49 two-door 39-seaters delivered to the Arriva Nederland fleet in 2000/01. (Sholto Thomas)

Between 1999 and 2002, BC Transit in Canada bought a number of Plaxton Pointer-bodied Dennis Darts with 33 seats, two doors, air conditioning and double-glazed windows. This one is in Victoria in 2018. (Keith McGillivray)

Autobuses Prisei of Madrid bought 12 of these 29-seat two-door Dennis Darts with Spanish-built Unvi bodies in 2000.

Right: A 2007 Dublin Bus Volvo Olympian B9TL with 93-seat Alexander Dennis Enviro500 body, at Heuston station in Dublin. (Sholto Thomas)

Below: Toronto-based Go Transit has a large fleet of Alexander Dennis Enviro500 SuperLo double-deckers, built to an extra-low height (12ft 10in, 3.91m) to allow them to operate throughout the North American continent. This is a 2016 81-seater at Toronto bus station in 2018. (Keith McGillivray)

Ritchies Transport provides services throughout New Zealand. This 2018 89-seat Enviro500 is operating on the Northern Express network of Auckland Transport.

Liveried for Leinster Rugby is a 2019 Aircoach Volvo B11R with Plaxton Panther 49-seat body, in Dublin in 2022. (Richard Walter)

AC Transit, with a large bus fleet based in Oakland, California, bought 15 of these 81-seat Enviro500s in 2019.

Right: PostAuto, the Swiss Post subsidiary that provides regional and rural bus services throughout Switzerland, invested in the European three-door version of the AD Enviro500 double-decker in 2017–19, and this 80-seat St Gallen bus is seen near Interlaken Ost. The Enviro500 Postbus variant has also been supplied as the basis for the substantial orders from the BVG of Berlin. (Keith McGillivray)

Below: For many export customers requiring high-capacity buses, the choice is often between articulated single-deckers and three-axle double-deckers. Here at Lausanne, Switzerland, in the fleet of Transports Publics de la Region Lausannoise, a Hess articulated trolleybus sits alongside a 79-seat three-door 2019 AD Enviro500. (Sholto Thomas)

Chapter 8
Alexander Dennis

When the Alexander Dennis cavalry rode to the rescue of Alexander, Dennis and Plaxton between 2004 and 2007, it inherited a few models that had been developed in their independent years, as well as some that had appeared as TransBus started to develop its range using Alexander, Dennis and Plaxton know-how.

When part of TransBus, Alexander and Dennis had been working closely together on the Enviro bus range. Under Alexander Dennis, this relationship now became even closer, although it was still possible to specify chassis from outside AD, notably Plaxton coach bodies on Volvo chassis, and while buses were almost inevitably complete AD products, some operators specified AD bus bodies on Volvo chassis. The industry had moved on conclusively from the previous UK norm, where operators ordered chassis from one builder and bodies from another, to a one-stop shopping process where it was easier to control quality issues and guarantee delivery times.

Many existing models had to be sacrificed as AD moved towards a range of efficient up-to-date models. Under Mayflower, the successful ALX range had started morphing into the new Enviro range, retaining the type numbers so that the ALX200 became the Enviro200 range of lighter-weight single-deck buses, and the two-axle ALX400 double-deck similarly became the Enviro400. These joined the full-size single-deck Enviro300, and the three-axle double-deck Enviro500.

The Alexander Dennis Enviro200 was a popular choice in London fleets. This 2008 First CentreWest 29-seat two-door example is at Golders Green in 2009.

Stagecoach Enviros in Northampton in 2014. The Rugby-bound bus is a 2009 46-seat Enviro300 on MAN 18.240 chassis, and the Daventry bus is a 2014 37-seat Alexander Dennis Enviro200.

An early diesel-electric hybrid, a 2009 London United Enviro200H two-door 29-seater in Richmond when new.

Biogas-powered Scania K270UB/Enviro300s were built in 2014 for Reading Buses and, as here in Sunderland in 2023, for Stagecoach. This is a 43-seater.

London fleets bought substantial numbers of the Enviro400. In Whitehall in 2012 is a 2006 two-door 67-seater for Go-Ahead's London General fleet.

Stagecoach was a major customer for the Enviro400 model. This a 2008 80-seat example working in Inverness in 2009.

Diesel-electric hybrids proved to be a bridge between diesel-engined and pure battery-electric buses. A 2011 Metroline 61-seat Enviro400H turns among London traffic into Oxford Street in 2014.

Although the Enviro500 was primarily an export double-decker, First bought 25 82-seat examples for its Glasgow fleet in 2009.

The Enviro300 was replaced by longer versions of the Enviro200 from 2017, and the Enviro500 is available in different versions to suit the requirements of export markets, so there are Asia Pacific, Europe, Latin America and North America variants, as well as the SuperLo and Enviro500EV CHARGE for North American customers.

The great majority of these have been complete AD vehicles, but the bodies could be, and were, built on other chassis. With the move away from diesel-engined buses, there grew a long list of variants. The Enviro200, for instance, was first introduced in diesel form in 2006, followed by the hybrid diesel-electric Enviro200H in 2009, the face-lifted MMC version in 2014, and the electric Enviro200EV (on BYD chassis) in 2016. MMC stood for Major Model Change, an internal project title that although widely used, never formed part of the product name.

The spin-offs from the Enviro400 range, which had been introduced in 2005, have been even more numerous. The Enviro400H hybrid followed in 2015, the electric Enviro400EV in 2018 in partnership with the Chinese manufacturer BYD – and there have been Smart Hybrids, Electric Range hybrids, the Enviro400FCEV double deck hydrogen-fuel cell bus from Alexander Dennis, an Enviro400CBG version on Scania biogas chassis and, on Volvo B8L chassis, the tri-axle XLB variant.

Alexander Dennis continued to build chassis at Guildford, but the Guildford plant closed in 2020 amid a severe market downturn, and chassis production was concentrated at a contractor in Leyland that had been offering extra capacity for years. The long-established engineering connection with south-east England is maintained at the new Trident House engineering development facility at Farnborough.

Plaxton today builds bus and coach bodies at its Scarborough plant, with new coach models developed to suit changing requirements in the touring and express coach markets. Today, Plaxton produces around 200 coaches annually, primarily for the UK and Ireland, but in recent years, sales have expanded into Europe and further afield to New Zealand. This is in addition to the buses produced at the Scarborough plant.

The restyled MMC version of the Enviro200 appeared in 2014. This 41-seat Enviro200, delivered to Stagecoach in 2016, passes extensive city centre redevelopment in Newcastle in 2023.

Two 2017 buses in the New World First Bus fleet in service in Hong Kong, a 31-seat Enviro200 followed by an 80-seat Enviro400.

A 2019 short-length 29-seat Enviro200 from the Edwards, Llantrisant fleet, in Treforest. (Sholto Thomas)

Coats of many colours worn by a line of First Glasgow AD Enviro buses – Enviro200 single-deckers and Enviro400 double-deckers in a bright selection of route-branded colours.

Stagecoach introduced a pilot service with an autonomous bus between Fife and Edinburgh in 2023 as part of Project CAVForth. This 2019 Enviro200 43-seater is one of five fitted with autonomous technology including cameras and sensors. There is a safety driver who can take full manual control when needed, as well as a bus captain to look after passengers boarding and buying tickets. (Richard Walter)

A BYD/AD Enviro200EV for Fullers Group operating on Waiheke Island in New Zealand for Auckland Transport. It is a 2020 two-door 33-seater.

Operators providing services for Transport for London have invested in BYD/AD Enviro200EVs, like this 2020 two-door 29-seater for Go-Ahead London.

A comparison of Enviro400 front ends in Manchester in 2016. On the left is a 75-seat 2014 First Enviro400, passing a restyled 77-seat 2016 Stagecoach Enviro400.

Waiting for passengers at its terminus at York railway station is a 73-seat 2020 East Yorkshire Enviro400 on the EastRider service, linking York with Hull. (Sholto Thomas)

Two 2020-delivered Enviro400s pose with Newcastle's iconic Tyne Bridge of 1928 in the background. The buses are 72-seaters in Go North East's Xlines livery.

In the centre of Leeds in 2022, a 2020 Enviro400 in Transdev's Harrogate Bus Company fleet operating the X99 service to Wetherby. (Richard Walter)

Enviro400s leaving Newcastle's Haymarket bus station in 2023 – a 2022 Arriva 73-seater followed by a 2016 Stagecoach 77-seater.

Nottingham City Transport's 100th gas bus in 2022, complete with suitable registration mark, is a 2019 Scania N280UD with Enviro400 72-seat body. (Sholto Thomas)

Enviro400ER double-deckers for Dublin Bus under construction at the Plaxton plant at Scarborough. The plants at Falkirk and Scarborough both build the AD bus range and Scarborough builds the Plaxton coach range.

Two Enviro400ER two-door 67-seaters, new in 2021, in Transport for Ireland livery for the Dublin Bus fleet.

National Express West Midlands has a growing fleet of AD buses. This is a 2018 Enviro400 SmartHybrid 73-seater liveried for the high-frequency 50 route.

Stagecoach East invested in three-axle Enviro400 XLBs for its fleet operating on the Cambridge guided busway in 2019. They are two-door 98-seaters.

The Enviro400 City body style was initially introduced for London operators, but it has also become popular around the country. Crossing Kingston Bridge in 2022 is a 2021 RATP Group electric BYD D8UR DD/Enviro400 City two-door 65-seater.

The electric BYD D8UR model with Alexander Dennis bodywork has become a popular choice with operators. These two 70-seat 2021 examples pass in the centre of Aberdeen in 2022. (Keith McGillivray)

McGill's Xplore fleet in Dundee includes BYD8UR/AD E400EVs like this strikingly liveried 2021 example seen when new. (Keith McGillivray)

Finished in the Bee Network livery adopted by Transport for Greater Manchester contracted services is a 2023 BYD D80UR/AD Enviro400EV 62-seater for the Go North West fleet.

Citybus in Hong Kong has a large fleet of Alexander Dennis buses; these are 2016 Enviro500 98-seaters.

Enviro500 double-deckers under construction at AD's North American plant at Nappanee, Indiana.

A 2021 three-door 69-seat Enviro500 for the Land Transport Authority in Singapore, which contracts services to four operators, in this case SMRT. (Phil Halewood)

BVG, the Berlin operator, has taken substantial deliveries of these AD Enviro500 double-deckers since 2021. This 2023 delivery, seen when new, is a three-door 71-seater. (Keith McGillivray)

A 2015 Trentbarton Volvo B11RT with Plaxton Elite 57-seat body leaves Derby bus station on the Red Arrow non-stop service to Nottingham. (Sholto Thomas)

Buses and coaches nearing completion at Plaxton's Scarborough plant in 2017 – an Enviro400 for London operation and two Stagecoach Elite-bodied Volvo B11RTs.

Above: Plaxton developed the Panther LE model for shorter-distance express services, with a low-floor front section and a raised portion over the rear axles. This is a 2018 Stagecoach 53-seat example on Volvo B8RLET chassis, leaving Dunfermline bus station in 2022.

Left: A 49-seat 2019 Plaxton Leopard interurban on Volvo B8R chassis for Lothian Country's Green Arrow fleet.

Stagecoach's round-the-clock Oxford Tube link with London uses Volvo B11RLETs with Plaxton Panorama 77-seat bodies. This 2020 delivery is the latest in a series of coaches that have carried the T55 UBE registration mark. (Sholto Thomas)

A shorter-length Plaxton Panther Cub 34-seat body on Volvo B8R chassis for Shiel Buses, Acharacle.

The current home market Plaxton coach body range comprises the long-running Elite (in normal-height and Elite i interdeck versions), the Leopard, the Panther family (Panther, Panther LE and Panther Cub) and the twin-deck Panorama.

Alexander Dennis has returned to Northern Ireland, opening a new base in Ballymena in 2019 as an engineering office. And in Scotland, the development site at Larbert, which had previously produced the prototypes of new models, was being redeveloped in 2023 to install production lines for AD's new Enviro400EV electric bus.

So the names of Alexander, Dennis and Plaxton live on, when once it looked as if they were ready to join a string of once-distinguished names consigned to the history books. In their long histories, Alexander, Dennis and Plaxton have had a great deal in common. The businesses founded in 1895 by John and Raymond Dennis, in 1907 by Frederick William Plaxton and in 1913 by Walter Alexander, were not initially created to build bus and coach bodies. Dennis made bicycles, Plaxton was a joinery business and Alexander was a fast-growing bus operator. Even though the three strands of AD went through many challenges in the 1990s and early 2000s, that they survive today as the main British bus and coach builders is testimony to sound management, an ability to anticipate market trends, attractive designs, well-built vehicles and a determination to succeed.

All of it has paid off by attracting substantial orders. The Enviro200 in its various guises has sold over 8,000 units, the Enviro400 range over 12,000 and the Enviro500 range some 6,000.

The most recent major episode in the story has been the 2019 purchase of AD by NFI Group, the Canada-based business. Founded in 1930, it is now the largest transit bus manufacturer in North America. In addition to Alexander Dennis and Plaxton, the group includes New Flyer, builder of transit buses, MCI, which builds coaches, and ARBOC, which specialises in 'cutaway' van conversions.

Under its new ownership Alexander Dennis continues to flourish, launching a new-look, new-generation range of AD electric buses in 2023 that are fully designed and built in-house. There is a return to smaller buses with the 8.5m-long Enviro100EV, plus the completely restyled Enviro400EV and Enviro500EV to complement the existing Enviro diesel ranges and the BYD-based electric models. The Enviro100EV and Enviro400EV are designed specifically for the UK and Ireland market.

Alexander Dennis can proudly state that its buses carry 25,000 passengers every minute of every day around the world, and in London alone its buses carry 3.5 million passengers per day. Around the world there are 31,000 Alexander Dennis buses and Plaxton coaches in service.

Trident House in Farnborough allows AD to retain an important presence in the south of England. This facility concentrates on new product development and zero-emission ambitions, as well as engineering and testing. Here, work is in progress on home- and export-market models.

One of the first deliveries of the new-look Enviro500 was this bus for KMB in Hong Kong, a long-established AD customer with early orders for Alexander bodies dating back to the 1970s.

AD released this image of its next-generation electric bus family for the UK market, consisting of the Enviro100EV, marking a return to smaller buses, and the Enviro400EV, which shares common styling features with the restyled Enviro500 export model. Both wear the new AD logo.

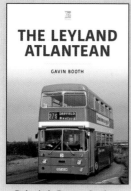
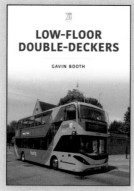
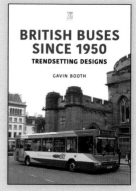
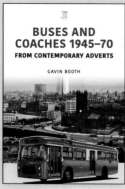
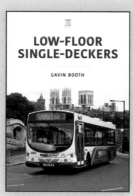